TRIUMPH HOUSE
Poetry with a Purpose

THE BREATH OF LIFE

Edited by

Steph Park-Pirie

First published in Great Britain in 2004 by
TRIUMPH HOUSE
Remus House,
Coltsfoot Drive,
Peterborough, PE2 9JX
Telephone (01733) 898102

SB ISBN 1 84431 067 1

Saint Michael's Church
Bishop Middleham

Written by
Susan Carole Gaol-Roberts
On page 14

FOREWORD

In today's modern world everyone's life is fast-moving and hectic, leaving little time to stop, open our minds and gather together our thoughts. However, there are times when we really do need to take time out to sort our feelings and emotions. Poetry can very often provide us much-needed release by allowing us to express and share our important thoughts with others.

The Breath Of Life is a special collection of these poems, featuring the work of over 120 new and established authors of today.

Together they combine their creative talents to present to you an inspiring and enjoyable read that you will want to return to time and time again.

Steph Park-Pirie
Editor

CONTENTS

DON'T ASK FOR WHOM JESUS WEEPS, HE WEEPS FOR THEE

It was I who drove the nails into Your hands,
And hoisted You onto that tree,
The one who made the seas and land,
The one who came to set me free.

But those five wounds have long since healed,
The crown of thorns turned to dust,
Now the awful truth to me revealed,
I'm ashamed to say it, but I must.

The nails and spears failed from the start,
For You are spirit not flesh and blood,
But we wounded You to the heart,
That did not heal nor ever could.

Your pain was not of nails' injection,
You who came down from Heaven above.
The pain was caused by man's rejection,
The ignoring of Your perfect love.

I cannot hurt Your limbs again,
You have ascended to Your Holy Throne,
But my indifference still causes You pain,
The guilt is mine and mine alone.

Please forgive me, I did not know,
Help me love You and heal Your heart,
I will tell others where ere I go,
You've won my love, and that's a start.

Bill Hayles

GO FORWARD, HEAVENLY LIGHT

O brave and tender twilight,
interposing stars and day;
Promises, all things bright

A fragrance of flower light
lining our way;
O brave and tender twilight!

Though passive dew might
dreams let drop away . . .
Promises, all things bright

Love, hope, lies made right
we pray;
O brave and tender twilight!

Let doubts, fears, in sight
stay out of harm's way;
Promises, all things bright

Black on black, white on white,
striking out per se;
O brave and tender twilight!
Promises, all things bright

R N Taber

JESUS HELP ME

Sometimes I lack patience . . . *Jesus help me!*
That I may keep all Your Commandments . . . *Jesus help me!*
When I feel lost and insecure . . . *Jesus help me!*
At times when tears saturate my pillow . . . *Jesus help me!*
Often I cannot see the answers to my problems . . . *Jesus help me!*
Put a seal on my tongue, when necessary . . . *Jesus help me!*
Should loneliness creep around my soul . . . *Jesus help me!*
When I find those I love, do not love me . . . *Jesus help me!*
Whenever I need a lover, comforter, friend . . . *Jesus help me!*
Give me strength to turn away from wrong doing . . . *Jesus help me!*
If I feel jealousy pangs, now and again . . . *Jesus help me!*
When I am laid low in spirit . . . *Jesus help me!*
To care for all Your creatures . . . *Jesus help me!*
There are times, when I feel sick and faint . . . *Jesus help me!*
I want to find Your lost sheep . . . *Jesus help me!*
As You love everyone . . . *let me do likewise . . .*
Jesus help me!

M Ross

TRUE LOVE (DAILY DEVOTION)

Devotion to God is
Truth and Love.

Truth without Love offends,
Love without Truth deceives.

Therefore,
Whoever wishes to grow
must strive to obtain true love.

This is life's central point
and the assurance of a constant inner growth.

Acknowledgement of true greatness
does not conflict.

There is only one cure for the highs
and lows of our inner life:
To be loved truthfully
This is God's way.

He is loving and charming,
He is confident.

Millions will read,
the true story of His life
and be enthralled.

Poets and musicians,
united to sing Him praises.

Unknown in life,
He is known to all mankind
Love and Divine.

We have to become
a little dart,
flaming with the fire of His Divine Love

So that it may pierce
the most inner depths
of our heart.

This is true love, full of divinity,
so appeasing and devoted.

Alexander Osunwoke

GOD MADE US ALL

As we move around each day,
Many other folk we see,
And as I pondered for a while,
This thought came to me.

Some folk are short, others tall,
Some are fat and others thin,
But then what really matters,
Is the heart within.

To God we are all His children,
So listen to His call,
No matter what our stature is,
We know He loves us all.

He gave us all a body,
Of which we should take care,
He also put a soul within,
We should sustain with prayer.

So as you go about your tasks,
That you have to do each day,
If you need the Maker's help,
Find the time to pray.

Not all prayers will be answered,
He never claimed they would,
But you can be sure of this,
Those answered are for your good.

Will A Tilyard

YOU SHINE

'You shine child,' the old lady said.
'Your smile lights up the night.
Pray tell why you appear by my bed.'

The youthful one replied,
'Do you remember yourself when a girl,
When like a flower you unfurled?
A wild child, the sun your guide,
When you ran through the woods,
Or along the oxtail waters of the canal.
You, as graceful as a comely swan,
Racing from your primary school,
On your way home to your mamma.
Then you looked the same as I,
Green with youth under a spring sky.
Now your youthful ways are gone.'

'I remember it well little stranger,
With you I sense no danger,
No more than I do of He,
Who long ago was born within a manger.
For my time here I know now is over,
As I return to the Elysian fields of clover.
For you my little angel and guardian,
So long in my dreams I have known,
Have come to take me to my heavenly home.'

Julia Pegg

UNTO US A CHILD IS BORN

The moon was low and full that day
A cold and damp winter's morn,
There in the hay, the oxen breath,
Gave warmth to a king, just born.

The mother Mary's task now done,
Took rest on Joseph's shoulder,
And in her eye a tear was found
Joy for her little Soldier

The donkey neighed; the silence gone
And the world rejected, full might.
With sin no longer held head high,
And the world is put to right.

'Jesus, my son,' the mother cried,
My heart is full of joy,
'I love you, little mite asleep,
My own sweet darling Boy.'

Ecstatic mother in her love,
With husband's joy to release,
They hugged the Child and wept with love,
Heaven and Earth in fullest peace . . .

Amen.

Paul Kelly

LIFE POEMS

I chisel diamonds for your souls,
My actors play so many roles,
Poems inspired by the Muses,
Portray my life-search and its bruises,
Necklaced pearls of tears and dew
Things I have felt, you feel them too,
Snapshots of moments eternally caught,
A diadem of love, tenderly wrought
An eagle soaring, a bolt from the sun
Lighting heart candles, one by one,
A star-speckled sky, a vision seen nightly
Divine orchestrations you cannot take lightly,
My poems come from various races,
From ancient lore and bygone faces;
A bridge through time, a dance that's immortal,
Of hidden dimensions, the secret, the portal,
Life's meaning, its jewel, its sense and core,
A poem's all that, but also much more,
A message from Heaven, a script writ in gold,
A witness from Spirit as humans unfold.

Emmanuel Petrakis

RAW LIFE

She's just a splinter
from a broken home
existing in enduring poverty
in a room dark as her sins.

Alone, confused and despondent,
pinched with hunger
smells pizza from nearby cafe
that invades quivering nostrils.

In contrast reaches for saucepan
and pygmy primus stove,
to unite cheap baked beans
with sauce like arterial blood.

Today monthly rent is due
'snake-eyed landlord' arrives,
to ogle youthful body
and moral conflict will soon be tested.

Lord help her out of the abyss
let gainful hire be legal
with wholesome smiles of content
to unfasten this raw life.

Alex Branthwaite

Is, Was And Always Will Be

In this life that is so perverse,
We need the comfort of Christian verse.

The rhyming hymn, the haunting prayer,
They hardly change and are always there.

The words we use will forever last,
Used by generations for centuries past.

As you give your all in your Sunday pew,
Few can remember when the words were new.

Words of comfort, suppressing fear,
Relevant as in yesteryear.

Your worshipping confidence will not collapse,
If you let your worship lapse.

T A Napper

SENTIMENTS

I don't want to be a cloud over your morning,
Or a stone inside your shoe,
I know you feel all the dreadful warnings,
And what this does to you.
I used to be your ray of sunshine,
That brightened up your day,
And somehow over a short space of time,
This has wilted away.
You used to love the way I smile,
And the silly things I do,
I made you laugh once in a while,
You made me laugh too.
I used to feel like your princess,
Now I feel like the pea,
All I cause you is distress,
In hoping you still love me.

Gail Whitcher

BRIGHT

(In loving dedication to the parents of Holly and Jessica)

Can such brightness decompose?
Surely not! And yet it did.
Oh, let us keep our children hid
In Christ who guards for evermore
Those bright smiles and
Our love for sure.

Deborah Shah

SAINT MICHAEL'S CHURCH, BISHOP MIDDLEHAM

High on a hill stands Saint Michael's church, old, majestic and proud,
Where God's congregations kneel in prayer and then stand to
                                                    sing aloud . . .
Running noses, old men coughing, people singing hymns out of tune,
At services and funerals, old croaking voices croon.
At Christenings hear the baby's cries above the organ playing,
At weddings couples vowing to love, with honouring and obeying.

Now my Saint Michael's stands locked by key,
And guarded by headstones and I cannot get in.
Once in years long ago, my sisters and I were free to go in and sing -
Three little girls' voices would resound, around those old stone walls,
Like a tiny choir in song, our private time to sing to God,
Where we were made to feel like we belonged.

The Reverend Mr Porteus, was the first vicar I remember,
What a good service he would perform, on a cold night in December.
He came to school to conduct a service and to say prayers,
We were blessed by him on a Monday morning . . .
And we all felt that he cared.

When my grandmother died, the hymn he chose that morning was -
'Dear Lord and Father of Mankind'.
I would sing this hymn with her
When I stayed with Grandmother at night.
It has been my favourite hymn ever since
And it will be for the rest of my life.

Most of my dear departed family, have had a service here,
In our old Saint Michael's church, we don't hurt or hold any fear . . .
Knowing they are all at rest alongside our Saint Michael's Church . . .
Held so fondly in our hearts, where they lie at our family's request.

In church have you ever watched children getting comfy on a pew?
And when you go to kneel in prayer, how the cushions always move?
In church do you listen for God, to whisper your name in calling?
I bet you would also turn around to see, thinking,
Who said my name, oh so quiet, so heavenly?

Oh Bishop Middleham, who holds the key,
To set our good Saint Michael's free?
Well, never mind, it's sad I know, but no matter where I live or go,
My old Saint Michael's church will, abide with me.

Susan Carole Gash-Roberts

MAJESTY ENTHRONED

I look up at the cross and what do I see?
The Saviour's blood, shed for me;
The Saviour's body all bruised and torn,
At the place where people come to mock and to scorn.

I look up at the cross and what do I see?
The Saviour's body broken for me;
A body sacrificed, so I might live
It's what the Saviour chose to give.

I look up at the cross and hear a voice cry out;
Cry out to the Father above.
My Saviour, the Lord has surrendered His soul
To display the fullness of His love.

I look up at the cross -
It is empty and bare;
My Lord is in Heaven
On His regal chair.

I look up at the cross,
It is surrounded by light;
The Lord watches over us
Both day and night.

'Sleep peacefully my child,'
He calls to me in my sleeping state,
'I will watch over you,
Until you awake.

I will continue to protect you
And support you through the day;
I will surround you and embrace you -
With my love you shall not fail.'

So I will look up at the cross, Lord
And continue to follow Your light.
I will embrace You as my Saviour,
The Lord of power and might.

Debbie Nobbs

ONWARD CHRISTIAN SLUMBER

Contraception everywhere; divorce;
A plague of porn;
And unremitting slaughter,
Every day, of the unborn.

And on the tide has swept.

Satan's friends and dupes
Have picked a winner citing 'choice'
In helping liberalism
Gain an efficacious voice.

In this they've been adept.

Christians, unmindful of
Their task to fight for right,
Have looked the other way
And let the dark replace the light.

In this they've been inept.

Supporters of permissiveness
Are now resolved to try
For legal euthanasia -
'Let people choose to die'.

So true to 'choice' they've kept.

As all this has continued,
And ever worse became,
Most Christians have done nothing
To oppose the mounting shame.

And on and on they've slept.

Anthony Hofler

COLOUR

Colour is a divine element
Enhancing basic shades
    Giving them enrichment
    On foundation that soon fades.

A beam of light divides
When shone through blocks of glass
    Refracting into rainbow hues
    In sequence as they pass.

An artist's palette can transfer
The various tints and paints
    On to a canvas and depict
    The shepherds and the saints.

And then we come to look at flowers
Their colours have no bound
    Whether strong or pastel shades
    Or poppies all around.

Who gave these colours which we love?
So many give delight
    Surely they come from Heaven above
    For mankind's keen insight.

R T James

JESUS CAME

Jesus Christ has come today . . .
a tiny Babe in a manger of hay.
Shining at night was a bright, Golden Star . . .
showing the way to kings from afar.

Shepherds in a field did abide . . .
while angel choruses covered the countryside.
Go and tell! Let the anthems swell . . .
Jesus Christ has come today.

Carol Olson

JESUS

An austere face
In such a vibrant role
The image does not fit.
Expanding thought
In times of need
In parables he did speak.
A discerning mind
A thoughtful gaze
Hands clasped
Problems solved.
People rose to greet
Then sat at His feet
Wisdom to be told.

John Hobbs

One Flesh Covenant

Wife,
This day I have
Chosen you as my
Companion in life.
Looking down the
Straits of time,
I have seen you
There with me.
I have seen love
And comfort as our
Travelling companions.
I have seen past
The dew of youth
To the changing seasons
Of our lives,
And I am satisfied.
This day I promise
That I will long
Be satisfied with
Your unfading smile,
The touch of your hand,
And the gift of your
Presence to me.

Husband,
This day I have
Chosen you as my
Companion in life.
I, too, have looked
Down the straits of time
And I have seen you
There with me.
I have seen you as a
Solid rock, always.

I have seen past
The dew of youth
To the changing
Seasons of our lives,
And I am satisfied.
This day, I promise
That I will long
Be satisfied with
Your unfailing courage,
The touch of your
Hand upon mine,
And the gift of your
Commitment to me.

. . . And they shall be one flesh
Genesis 2:24

Alice Parris

PUDDLE FUN

Seeing the rain, I leapt outside.
Lifted my face
and laughed with the sky.

Others scuttled for shelter,
under coats and roofs,
cursing their open-toe shoes.
Whilst I ambled
and sang
and thanked.

Meeting my friend
who was doing the same,
we ran with a laugh
and a prayer
up the street.

Puddle fun,
free from plastic macs,
umbrellas and yellow wellies.
We invented our game
of jumping in with both feet.

The solemn drivers
cursed and crawled
in jams
at our heels,
as we skipped alongside
with squelches and squeals.

Nothing so perfect
as enjoying the world,
stand up
and let the fun unfurl.

Sara Campbell-Kelly

WHAT IS TIME?

Time is colours in the sunrise,
Time is birdsong shrill and clear.
Time is a starting of the new day,
Time is knowing you are near.

Time is always in the future,
Time is always in the past.
Time is living for the moment,
Time is sweet memories that last.

Time is waiting for the future,
Time is healing from the past.
Time is frozen in the horror,
Time is the moment that will last.

Time is precious with the lover,
Time is halted with the kiss.
Time is the smile from the mother,
Time is new birth, baby bliss.

Time is the messages of sorrow,
Time is the hurting and the pain.
Time is hoping for the morrow,
Time is when living starts again.

S K Morgan

DAVID

David, dear David, my heart bleeds for you,
Shattered in disbelief,
Devastated beyond tears,
Dazed as though your head had hit a wall,
Every fibre of your being
Aching in pain,
Stretched to the maximum.
It is now spent -
The hurt remains and will not go away.

One minute, 'All is well,' you say,
Then comes the cloud,
The sun is blotted out,
A heavy tiredness grips you in its grasp.
You want to sleep
Then want to wake again,
Restless you move from this to that,
This moment eager just to talk and talk,
The next an urge to hide and meditate.

These days are not the worst,
All of us know.
The time will come when you will feel alone,
When family, friends and all have scattered far.
I have no fears for you
For you have faith
In One who never yet has let you down,
The One your dear one now sees face to face.
In this way you are ever close to her.

Kathleen Davey

UNTITLED

A small, war-time farm on a Sunday morning
Sunday roast in the oven
Collecting eggs by the dozen
Farm horses grazing in the field
Farmer sizing up his yield
Pigs a-grunting in cleaned out sty
Ducks a-splashing in pond nearby
Hens scratching freely in the old stackyard
Farm dog sleeping in shade of barn
And as I gaze at clear blue sky
The world seems at peace
And so do I.

Dorothy Kershaw

EVENING STILLNESS

Sitting in a garden chair
evening stillness drops gently onto warm summer air,
and with it disappears the noise -
and hurly-burly of our busy lives.
It all just fades away,
packed up and gone home,
leaving behind a quietness that can induce
a pleasant drug-like sleep.

In the distance, hear the sweet warblings
of birds in conversation,
their chatter and song as sweet as any poet's verse.
Trees swaying in a light breeze,
fans all in its path.
Let it wash over us, this stillness
and refresh us;
make us ready for a welcome slumber
and then - a brand new day.

Lynda Arnold

BROKEN TOOL

Let us say
This broken thing is actually complete,
Made for a purpose that was once unknown.
The path that drops into the sea
Because the cliff edge crumbled,
Leads in fact to flight;
For if I had not fallen
I would not have known
My flailing arms were wings.

Susan Latimer

CRANESBILL

If the clouds above your head,
Like the islands of the blest
Move and change eternally;
Does not the sun
With clear untrammelled light
Through your petals,
Blue, soft-veined in white
Create the heavens in your heart,
As if creation came to live
Within the compass of your flower.
While stars and sun, wheel and burn
In endless space above my head,
Move to unknown unspoken destinies,
Into the depths of that blue world I look
See the stamens touch the air
That passes where it will,
And know that all things made
From old and from tomorrow's dawn,
Are painted here, and you in them appear
In one gigantic marriage
Of daring skill and loving care.

K K Bolton

LINES TO HIS WIFE

Let me be old, Madam, let me be old.
Permit my beard to grey a little;
My hand to tremble, just the slightest bit,
My eye to be less sure than I pretend it is.

Allow the hairs upon my head to thin;
My memory to fail me now and then;
My thoughts be more concerned with peace,
And less concerned with life's great mysteries.

Let me admit I criticize the young;
Let me despair that only I am wise;
Then let me know, above all else,
That comforts we together yet may find
In pleasing one another, these will abide.

Alex Anderson

SPIRIT AND SOUL

They say, spirit
      and soul
can make the feeling
      of emotion so whole.
Make you feel hope
make you feel love
      and also believe
      in faith too.
The coldness you
      can sometimes feel
is it the feeling
      the emotion?
      No one loves me.
Oh Lord! No one loves me.
But the spirit
      and soul
in the end
      will always grab hold
and the pressure relieved
      is by tenfold.
And your spirit
      you feel
oh yeah! You feel
      feel like gold
spirit and soul.

P S Davidson

A Writer's Poem

Don't go (back) till everything's alright (?)
in this night, (He) teacheth me t'write, and
(His) hand upon, my shoulder - bright; fanned
into Love, mine heart o'fire - with, light we are manned
as, across the sand of time - we flow both day and night!

Be at rest, yes! Rest in (Him), thru all yer days
and - in His hand, also cometh (His) praise
for tho we be, both small 'n' (sometimes) crazed
yet - (He) faithful - be.

(His) sée
stretches near 'n' far - for (all) to grasp
and in our ways, we find (His) - kinda! Task
to enter into love.
(He) reigns!

Oh Jesus, Your 'n' holy strains
in us as we walk 'n' talk
'n' handle one another
like Your mother, sister, brother!
                              Amen.

Anon

SOUNDS OF MUSIC

Cheep, cheep of birds
    in leafy canopies green,
Sweet warbles heard
    wafted along on summertime breeze.

Trees, tall, slender
    caw, caw of rooks
Cascading waters
    coo of dove in shady nooks.

Frothy, wavelets tossing high
    ebb and surge
Sandy beaches stretching nigh
    butterfly wings, flap of birds flying by.

Nightingale's song of rapture
    in twilight peace and chorus at dawn
Honeybees' nectar sweet to capture
    breezes dancing midst golden, rustling corn.

Nature's creation for mankind
    gifts from above
Sounds breathtaking
    freely given, with His love divine.

Ivy Lott

A Cup Of Tea

I thought I'd put the kettle on and make a cup of tea,
But I'd like a friend to call awhile and share this time with me,
A friend to sit and talk awhile, to tell my troubles to,
But all is quiet, no one knocks, of friends I've but a few.

I sat awhile to drink my tea in the quietness of my room,
Then the sun came out, warmth spread around and took away
                                                    the gloom.
I felt someone sit near to me and whisper in my ear -
'I'm here with you, we'll sit and talk, you've nothing now to fear.

I am your friend, just sit awhile, just sit and sip your tea,
Then talk to me and reminisce, I'll listen patiently.
Please don't forget, you talk to me each time you kneel in prayer,
I've helped you through your troubles and your joys I always share.

I'm by your side, you're not alone when friends forget to call,
Just sip your tea, sit back, relax and let the teardrops fall.
Have I not been right by your side since you took me in that day?
Did I not promise to stay near you, not only when you pray?'

So I talked about not feeling well and all the aches and pains,
I told about the wrongs I do and my ill-gotten gains.
Of loneliness, of confidence that's always leaving me,
Of friends I know, but do not call, to help me drink my tea.

He then said He'd known me as a babe, He'd held me on His knee,
He picked me up when I fell down, He smiled to comfort me.
He held me close when loved ones died and kissed me tenderly,
And through the grief when I felt pain He gently carried me.

We talked and talked, the morning passed, He is a friend indeed,
He listened as I talked to Him and then we both agreed
That when I put the kettle on, in future I would see
A friend come in and stay awhile and help me drink my tea.

J Jones

THE WONDER OF NATURE

The sense of wonder and awe one perceives,
As a little child runs through the rustling leaves,
of reds and yellows, greens and rust,
the freedom to let go, and simply just trust.

Twirling and swirling the leaves whirl around,
Gently, whispering they fall to the ground.
The beauty of nature is a wonderful gift,
To take a little time out, gives the heart a big lift.

The trees are a variety of different shapes and sizes,
They are full of hidden treasure and life's surprises,
They reach out their arms open wide,
To give their love they hold deep inside,
The simplicity of a loving hug,
Two hands of a child wrapped around many a bug.

To see the birds fly freely, and open their wings,
This is one of the joys that autumn brings,
It is a joy to watch the children play,
To have a good time and enjoy the day,

To say thank you God is a simple prayer,
For the world of nature, Your love, Your care.

Tracey McConnell

REFLECTION

This face I see is not mine,
In the mirror, a puddle or pond,
My face is young, and soft, with clear fine skin,
And deep blue eyes that look within.
It's full of laughter with a saucy grin.
My new, young world, the start of my life,
Without worries, fear, pain or strife.
This face that I see is not really mine,
In my heart and my mind, my true face will shine
And people will see that age is a mask after all.

Averil D Carpenter

DOWN BY THE SEA

Thoughts of You my God fill my heart
As I stroll down by the sea
I long for You and You alone
To my heart You hold the key

I hear the sound of the surging waves
Dashing towards the shore
My Jesus, my God, my Lord, my life
How can I love You more?

The sunlight glints across the waves
Splashing on the sand
In You all my dreams converge
And Your will is my command

The beauty of the white spray flying
Upon the deep blue sea
But nought in all the world to compare
With the love You've shown me

Joan Magennis

PRIORITIES

What is important to you in life?
Is it being a woman, a man, or a wife?
Is it how many exams you have passed?
How you always came first and never came last!
Is it very important how much money you own?
Do you love it so much that you count it alone?
Life has so many treasures for us to acquire:
Some can be bought; some are on hire.
But life's greatest gift - the big dividend,
There isn't a doubt - it must be 'a friend'!
A friend always supports you, on days that are dark
Is there to share with you your latest, mad lark.
A friend is a pillar in life's bagatelle;
To have lived it without one would sure have been Hell!
So, whether you're rich or whether you're poor,
Count your blessings in *friends* and your world is secure.

R Humphreys

God's Eternal Love

In my imagination I look back over time
I see the Lord's creation, the firmament sublime
I see Him raise the mountains to their majestic heights
I see Him cutting valleys and coursing water rights

I see Him make the oceans, and the beautiful terrains
I see Him plant the woodlands and stretching out the plains
And then I see Him pausing and reflecting on the scene
And now I see Him placing man in that unspoiled domain

But sadly, sin was introduced when Adam disobeyed
And soon the thorns and weeds sprang up, depravity displayed
This didn't take God by surprise, He knew that man would sin
As He looked down through years of time and planned His own to win

The Bible tells us long before He made the planets move
He had decided to show forth the depths of His great love
By sending His Son down to Earth to die that man might live
Oh, how great His love for us, His only Son to give

God's love for us is so profound, it's hard to comprehend
It reaches down to where we are, our broken lives to mend
Eternal life made possible, to dwell with Him above
And a new standing with our God, whose very name is Love

So what are your responses to this redeeming love
Have you confessed your sinnership, got new life from above
Are you living in obedience to His Word and His Commands
Are you looking for His soon return and the bright and better land

K Craig

You Said

You said beauty, and not ashes,
You said joy for those who mourn,
You said, 'Child you are so precious,
For a purpose you were born.'

You said, 'Freedom for the captives,'
You spoke peace in times of strife,
You said, blessed are those who seek You,
In dark places You spoke life.

You said patience, not frustration,
You spoke purity, not shame,
You said, 'Child, I love you always,
In my hand I've carved your name.'

You said goodness, love and mercy,
When by sinning I was driven,
When I knelt before You broken,
You said, 'Child, you are forgiven.'

Polly Cordell

THE MIRACLE OF MOTHER NATURE

The creativity of life is so unique,
That's when Mother Nature reaches her peak,
It's the best possible thing that she can do,
That's create life like me and you
And we both know that on this Earth,
There's no more precious thing than birth,
Worth more than silver, more than gold,
Something special in love we hold,
A human life cannot be sold.

So think before you plant a seed,
Do you have everything you need,
To give your child happiness,
If you think the answer's yes,
Then proceed in developing your child,
Why not let Mother Nature run wild,
To give us things we could only dream,
To give us life just so supreme,
I just cannot start to believe,
This masterful art that we receive,
With open arms every day,
To the Lord up above I pray,
To keep this world nice and safe,
To keep this world a happy place
And give us yes, what we deserve,
A chance to enjoy another birth
And fulfil the dreams of our universe!

Andrew Chadfield

GOD'S HANDIWORK

From whispering grass and rustling tree,
spirit voices speak to you and me,
preserve this beauty if you can
it is the gift of God to man.

A sunrise pink on sparkling rills,
a flock of sheep on blue-tinged hills,
a valley ripe with golden corn,
silver cobwebs on a frosty morn,
a blackbird's song the heart doth thrill,
a host of golden daffodils.

'Tis our task to pass it on,
to generations yet unborn
and then our spirits can soar free
to whispering grass and rustling tree.

Stewart Davison

LULLABY

My helpless child, do not struggle to find me, I am here.
My weary babe, rest in my arms.
I know how you question and frantically scratch the surface of life
To see what hidden treasures dwell beneath the superficial dross,
And how your tears fall when your discovery is only more questions.
But cherished child will you rest for a while? Will you rest and know,
For the times when you struggle to carve out your way
Know that your path is already worn by my feet.
My way is not hidden from you as the road I have chosen to walk is
that of your life.
For the times when to walk jars and aches, when you stumble and fall,
See my nail-pierced hands stoop tenderly to my sheep,
See me hold the worn and weary on my back,
Hear my promise *I will carry you.*
For the times when your past ghosts haunt you,
Remember that *I am* not *I was.*
For the times that others' cruelty and harsh words burn you, melt you,
break you,
Hear me whisper, *blessed are the peacemakers, you are a child of mine.*
For the times your Jordan roars and threatens to destroy,
Know that your land of Canaan is only a step of faith away,
My mighty hand will dry the surging river, you will not drown.
For the times you can only feel the deep pain of thorns,
Remember they will reveal a flourishing rose.
For the times when you fear you do not know me at all,
Know there is no need to strain to hear my voice, it dwells in the beat
of your heart.

For all the times you will know
Listen, listen child to what is there
Hear my sweet melody as I sing over you,
As this Father delights in His child.

And may it be a gentle lullaby to your ear, to your bruised heart,
To your bursting, beautiful, baffled heart.
And may you, my child, know you are loved beyond what you
                                                    can know,
And rest in my everlasting arms.

Janette Kay

UNTITLED

Help me understand, Lord,
The sorrows of this world,
Let me understand, Lord,
The cruelty and crime,
It buries itself
Confusing my mind.
Are there answers, Lord,
To the questions I ask?
I don't understand, Lord,
The reasons I lack.
I pray for solutions
To the confusion and pain,
Help me understand, Lord
I ask You again.

E M Gough

A Prayer For Marion
(Written less than two months before she died)

There's nothing You don't know, O Lord
Of our pain and of our loss;
The tender love You have for us
Is what took You to the cross.

But what You gained is richer still
And far outweighs the pain,
For though You bore it all alone,
You are with us - and remain.
My helplessness is clear to me,
But I cannot doubt Your power
To comfort and to strengthen,
Every minute, every hour.

The visions and the dreams You give
Will surely be fulfilled,
As every tear is wiped away
And every storm is stilled.
The friend that You have given me
Is dearer every day;
What a precious joy it is to know
It will always be that way.

You have made our converse sweeter
And answered every prayer,
Bringing laughter's unique medicine
And lightening our care.
So may we never doubt, Lord,
Your ability to give,
In this place of earthly sorrow,
The chance to really live.
So, when I think of You, dear friend,
I know a joy that cannot end.

Jane Clay

TIMES LIKE THIS

It's at times like this when the water rises higher
And the sky above is darkening to black,
When the wind around me pulls at my clothes;
That's when I lose sight of my goal.

It's at times like this when my fear leaps up
And my heart is weak and afraid,
When there's never lights at the ends of tunnels;
That's when I'm lost and alone.

It's at times like this that I start to sink
And I know drowning is near,
When the waves rise up ready to fall -
That's when I come close to losing it all.

It's at times like this that I turn to You
Reaching out to grasp Your hand
Knowing if I but have the faith
Then I will be saved today.

It's at times like this that I want to shout
Hosannas to the highest height,
When I want to tell the world what You've done;
But I can't speak through my tears of joy.

It's at times like this when the water rises higher
And tumult is all around,
There in the storm walks my Saviour;
Commanding me to leave my boat.

J E Alban

TRUST IN JESUS

Trust in our Lord Jesus each day
He will be with you, when storms are at bay
When the winds are boisterously high
He will meet you, way past the vast sky

God will meet your every need
And will be a good friend indeed
Even, when the lightning flashes by
No need to worry, or give out a sigh

The Lord will be with you, to see you through
He, who calms the storms, that are in view
The storms will disappear, the winds will cease
For God is a gentleman, who brings the peace

When we look up, and pray to God above
He will answer, with His abundant love
Faith is the way, through His countless blessing
Even when our thoughts, are still a-wondering

Even when our faith is small
God is precious and loves us all
So when our thoughts seem to drift far away
Trust in Jesus, this gift is the way

Jean P McGovern

TAKE A GLANCE

Take a glance out of my windowpane,
You will agree there's lots to gain.
The view is glorious where I live,
The world has so much to give.
This is a wonderful time of year,
There's always so much to cheer.
'Tis summertime once again,
With so much sun and not much rain.
Daisies, buttercups and green grass dancing in the breeze.
Lots of green leaves blowing on the trees.
The sun sits high up in the blue sky,
Just a few white fluffy clouds passing slowly by.
Opening the door to a breath of fresh air,
Makes our life worthwhile, I do declare.

C M A Hughes

A Tribute To Kerry

In my lonely moments I've been thinking of Kerry,
With a heartache that only loving feelings can heal
I can see her face on my mind so plainly
With love in my heart for her memory I feel.
Remembering our words as we chatted together,
While drinking coffee in a West End cafe.
Each word and sentence was so sweet and so happy,
What great force of nature brought us so near.
I see her face in the first light of morning
Her voice seems to whisper in the breeze 'mong the trees.
With a smile like the warmth of the bright sun at midday
And a heart like the gold of the sunset at eve.
These sweet memories haunt me when I am lonely
Or when I'm disturbed by life's problems and cares,
When the autumn rain leaves its tears on the window
Or the dew leaves its tears on the trees in the park,
The memory doesn't fade like the shadows of evening
Nor the mist disappearing with the rays of the sun.
When I think of times that we were together,
I often feel lonely, but never alone.

James McIlhatton

APPROACHING AUTUMN

It's a cool September morning,
The day awakens in the flourishing sun,
Everything seems in a foggy apron;
Autumn is approaching,
And that is apprehended
In all mellowed features of fruitfulness!
Leaves of trees, forests all growing
Brown, are often shorn off
Under gusts of wind and rain,
Pink-yellow fruits like apples, plums, grapes,
All maturing to a ripened stage,
Make the boughs bend down
Under heaviness of juicy contents!
Fields seem almost laden
With golden yellow crops, weighing
Down almost to the ground!
The sun has just emerged
With a bright illumination yellow red
Spread all over the east horizon!
A big, dark eagle stately perched
On a distant craggy hill
Suddenly catches my eyes;
His big wings become tinged
With the cherished golden beams
That make them shine out
With a strange gleam of splendour
At the moment of his slow settling!

Something majestic the bird assumes,
He keeps on observing:
Mother Earth represents wholesome autumn
She is the cause of all sweet manifestations
In nature - so full of love, beauty and wonder!
There is enough of hopefulness and blessedness
For the feeling generations of man!

Kalyan Ray

THE SATURDAY TREAT

Oh how I looked forward to that day
It was the best day I ever had
My weekly penny
From my dad.

I had to walk a good two mile,
To our village shop,
Where I would buy a sherbet dab
And a lollipop.

P Block

CONFIDENCE

When I was young, I wished to write clearly,
So that everyone could understand.
So I, slowly and laboriously,
Copied text from copperplate writing books.
Other people's words.

When I went to work in a library,
I learnt the names of authors and their works.
I showed people where to find books,
What to find in them.
Other people's words.

Later in life, I worked in the office of a big company.
I typed letters and took minutes at meetings.
Other people's words.

Now I am older, I have the time to write - letters to my friends,
Joking, sympathising, describing life in the country,
Poetry or short stories for my own pleasure or that of my family.
Now I have made the words my own.

Penny Allwright

REFLECTIONS

Reflections, those quiet pools of thought
Wherein our true selves lie,
To comb, in dreamy calm, life's strands
And catch our mirrored eye.

Jennifer Cox

CONTENTMENT

Why dwell on anything that's sad?
You haven't got the things you had
When you were young, in love and cosy
And everything in life was rosy.
Be happy that you had it all,
Your children growing strong and tall . . .
Much later, in the way of things,
They naturally spread their wings.
Your partner died, you're on your own,
But never, never feel alone,
For those you love are seldom far,
Their love uplifts you like a star
And all your memories remain
To keep you happy, calm and sane.

Janet Leitch Bowerman

A Friend In Need

When upon my chair I sit
Have a cup of tea or knit
Do a jigsaw, read a book
Or at the television look
There are many things that I can do
To pass a fleeting hour or two
But sometimes, as I live alone
I feel completely on my own

I have a super family
Who always love and care for me
They'll rush to me at full speed
If ever I'm in desperate need
I do feel blessed beyond degree
Because they're always there for me

I have another friend you know
Who cares for me when I am low
If you, like me, live on your own
Don't just sit there all alone
Meet my friend who's always there
Offer up a silent prayer
And you will find as I have done
My God is there for everyone.

Dorothy Jones

ABRAHAM AND ISAAC
(Genesis chapter 22 and Hebrews chapter 11, verse 19)

So Abraham arose and took his journey
    To where the mountains of Moriah rise,
And in his brain those words of God were burning:
    'Take now your son, your Isaac whom you love,
Up to the mountain I shall tell you of,
    And offer him to me, a sacrifice.'

And so they went, the two of them together,
    The old man plodding on with feet of lead,
The young one puzzled, questioning his father:
    'Here is the fire, my father, here the wood,
But where the lamb for offering to God?'
    'God will provide a lamb,' the old man said.

Isaac was trussed and bound for offering,
    Isaac was laid upon the criss-cross wood.
Who then endured the deepest suffering:
    Isaac who saw the ending of his life,
Abr'am who raised the disinheriting knife
    To slay his son, obedient to his God?

Praise for the angel voice, praise for the ram
    Caught in the thicket by its curling horns;
Praise for the faith of godly Abraham
    Who knew that God could raise his son from death -
He who gave Adam, first of men, His breath;
    Praise that the Son from saving death returns.

P D Lawrence

GARDENS OF THE SPIRIT

Soft days, calm nights, balmy mists
point to nature's noble order,
rolling back to the great beginning
when harmony was the order of the day.
Well before the bruising came
in the walled-in garden of the Lord
there beauty shone, peace reigned
'til the serpent's sting bit in so deeply
that all was thrown into instant disarray.
Falling fast, falling far, bringing down
the scaffold of contentment,
sneaking in the undergrowth,
wildernessing the neatly crafted soul.

A costly antidote was bought
with agony and bloody sweat
in the garden of the olive press
on the slopes of *Dominus Flevit*.
Redemption's energy coming off
the rugged bough of high Golgotha.
A tree of life and healing for those,
who writhe beneath the serpent's sting.
Such grace gives instant ease
with hope of fresh togetherness at
the omega point of blissful consummation.
In the garden of paradiso
the last Adam takes his place,
circled with the friends of God,
harmony restored, creation out of exile
the lion and the lamb lie side by side,
righteousness and peace embrace.

R Dunlop

FOCUSED

Lord, may my mind be focused right on *You,*
Not trying to make do
With countless things I feel
And think;
A bit like Martha - maybe worse - when she prepared that meal.

Lord, help me to make sure I'm trusting *You,*
Not trying to make do
With trusting in my own ability
To trust;
A bit like Peter - maybe worse - when he walked on the sea.

Elma Heath

ABRAHAM

(Abraham believed and hoped, even when there was no reason
for hoping, and so became 'the father of many nations' -
Romans ch 4, vs 18)

A father of nations?
Is that what you were told
as you stood there, childless,
like a dry tree, old and
creaking in the cold
of your constant winter,
trying to stir life's sediment up
into the liquid of each new morning?
Your wife, four score and more,
did wait for life's flicker
deep inside an empty core?
Okay, Father Abraham,
I'll put down this pen
and you tell me again, and again and again . . .

Mark Halliday

PRAYER FOR STRENGTH

God give me strength
When I am weak
In body or in mind.
God give me strength
To see the way
And leave my fears behind.
God give me strength
To face today
When tomorrow seems so bleak.
God give me strength
To do Your will
Your blessings Lord I seek.

Jackie Graham

GUARDIAN ANGEL

What is this sight we behold?
Golden hair with a halo to match.
An angelic face of beauty.
Smiling lips that ease this weary soul.
Eyes that give out gentle loving care.
Hands that heal this wounded heart.
The white robe flowing in the breeze.
Wings supporting this heavenly body.
Calming all in despair.
All dark shadows cast aside.
Happiness and love in their place.
She is always near when needed.
My friend from God on high.
By my side forever to be
My guardian angel.

Norman Andrew Downie

THE COMING

A rainbow formed an arc between Heaven and Earth
A new beginning, a chosen one was given new birth
A master, bringing truths from the wise
Glory be, lift up thine hearts and rise
As stars twinkle in the darkest of night
This birth will give Mother Earth new light
Love growing stronger with the years
Taking away all our earthly fears
As He walks, as He grows, His love will pave the way
For children to live in peace at the dawn of each new day.

Marie Graham

HE IS HERE

My pain and I were all alone,
we hid ourselves within our home
I felt I had no one to care,
the tears then flowed as I felt despair.
Then I looked thru my windowpane
and sweet assurance to me came.
The branch was tapping, tapping clear.
Tapped out the comfort, 'God is here'.
I told Him how I felt today,
asked if He would take my pain away.
He gave me comfort, gave His grace,
and strength for all that I must face.
And in the whispering breezes clear
He told me He was always here.
So I lay quiet in my darkened room
and knew I had no room for gloom.
As long as He is here with me
I can, in truth, say 'Glory be!'
In all the times that I have cried
how swift His comfort to my side.
I know I have no one in view
but I do have someone very true.
He gives a sign to say He's here
then my scalding tears just disappear.
A gift I find He gives to me.
So I lie quiet - *patience see!*
All pain shall one day go away
this He told me when He came to stay . . .
                              O Lord!

Rosie Hues

THE LAST ONE TURN OUT THE LIGHT

Last night God turned out the moon
And told the sinner, 'I'm coming soon.
Tell my people time to get a grip
Next time it is the Earth I will eclipse
Like putting out the moon's light
I have every sinner in my sight.'
The planets did form St David's star
Yet every day you push God too far.
The moon reflects the light of the sun
To show all the universe God is number one.

Flames they came here from the sun
To show God's people what they have done
Sent from God with His great power
Turn off phone and weapons in a light shower.
Did you see what God can fix?
His angels did the same in nineteen sixty-six.
Those who follow the Devil God will fight
Like a switch He will turn out our light.
If you're a sinner there is lots to fear
Will you be the last one who is here?

Colin Allsop

PILOTS

Matthew, Mark, Luke, John
approaching Christology
North, South, East and West.

Norman Bissett

Untitled

John the Baptist
Born six months before the Lord
Baptising rich and poor
And then put by Herod
To the sword
To live in Heaven
For evermore
The sweet son of Elizabeth
Who paved the way
For Christ the Lord.

David A Bray

I PRAY

In my thoughts
In my words
In my head
In my heart
In my soul
In my mind
For all mankind
I pray!

Theresa Hartley

FREE TO KNOW THE FATHER'S HEART

Praise the Lord for a brand new start
For the wiped clean slate of a blood-washed heart.
The freedom of knowing the price is paid,
The debt is gone; you're not a slave.

Pick up your mat. Walk tall again
In a holy life now free from sin.
Forget the past and all its shame.
Don't live in fear, Christ took your blame.
The future now looks bright for you:
You can live, as God wants you to.

You are free to seek His face alone:
To stand in grace before God's throne.
Look at your clothes they are now gold,
Christ's interceding so be bold.

Come dance and sing. You please the King.
Or let falling tears be your offering.
Whisper now your joys and woes.
Your Father cares, you're a child He chose.
Climb upon His royal lap and listen.
Your Father speaks love not criticism.
Know He wants what's best for you,
He's on your side. His love is true.

So do not strive to win God's heart,
You've had that place right from the start.

R M Ellett

WONDERFUL WORLD

Heavenly Father, thank you for this beautiful world we live in
and all the wonderful things around us.

We must not take it for granted, help us to be aware,
of the effect we have on it, the general wear and tear.

Help us to be sensitive, alert and wise, about all that we can do,
whether it big or small, the effort will ensue.

For the protection of all you have given us, we need to make a fuss,
also, especially too, for the Lord Jesus.

L M L

ON THE PASSING OF A LOVED ONE

She lay peacefully sleeping,
Yet was not unaware
Of the hands in her keeping,
The night watchers there.

Sometimes in her eyes
Recognition still shone;
Then a sequence of sighs
And the moment was gone.

Now with love and remembrance,
Don't dwell on the sad,
But celebrate her living
And the good times she had.

In a field of sun-kissed flowers,
In pure radiance of light,
The everlasting hours
Oust the nothingness of night.

Her Lightened soul to God ascends,
Borne on the powerful wings of friends.

L E Growney

JESUS OUR FRIEND

Rest in me a while
and I will renew your strength
Sit with me a while
and I will allay your fears
Walk with me, talk with me
and let us listen to each other
Lay with me
and let us think
Upon victories won
Victories still to come
and of those that may seem lost
But trust in me
Have faith in me
For I am your friend
Your joy, is my joy
Your grief, is my grief
Your pain, my pain
Just turn your head
For *I am* there
Your life to share.

Jenny Minor

UNTITLED

We try to convey to each generation,
An understanding of ourselves
And knowledge from long ages
Of our friend and guide.

Learning of Jesus, we begin to grow
With inner feelings, we begin to know;
Centring hearts on love and peace -
Hear the teachings of the Lord!

The Lord can turn us around
From doubting mind, discontented heart
From our soul's confusion;
For in needing Him, He is by us.

With strength and humility He lived,
Leading us to forgiveness
Live by sharing His gift of love;
Love by sharing in his sacrifice.

A J Brooking

DELEGATION

Lord, you gave me a job to do,
And You and I together Lord, we did it well,
And in my quiet moments in the evening,
I said, 'Thank You,' and felt the comfortable satisfaction
Of a task completed,
Not perfectly, but better than I thought was possible when I began.

And when the time was right, I gave up cheerfully,
I placed the work in other hands to carry on my vision.
How pleased and proud I'd be, to see my expectations
And my ideals moved on, towards their merited conclusion.

But now, I can't believe it Lord!
I really can't believe that all I worked for,
Strove for, my hopes, my aspirations, should be rejected, wasted
(Not contemptuously but simply through the inability of she
Who followed me to grasp the measure of the undertaking).

I rage, I rail, I weep till spent, and in the silence a small voice whispers,
'Child, you need to talk to one who also had a job entrusted to Him,
Like yours, it had to do with loving people,
With spreading truth and vital information,
With helping each fulfil his true potential,
With helping each to plumb life's deeper meaning.
Like you, He did it rather well and when it was accomplished
Passed it on, so others could continue.
Like you, He watched His life work founder
Upon the weaknesses of human frailty.
Like you, He knew frustration, anger, desperation,
The waste of time and effort and misunderstanding,
(And His remit included hanging on a cross and suffering
Excruciating agony . . .)

Child, I gave you a job to do
And you and I together, we did it as well as you were able.
That is all I ask.'

Eleanor Bird

WHERE'S YOUR FAITH?

Where's the action of your faith
While sitting in your chair?
Where's the action of your faith
At your television stare?

Where's the commitment of your faith
When action is desired?
Where's the commitment of your faith
Don't you feel inspired?

Where's the courage of your faith
When you enter the unknown?
Where's the courage of your faith
Do you think you're on your own?

Where's the trust of your faith
At times of fear and doubt?
Where's the trust of your faith
When there's always help about?

Simon Martin

I Am

I am the door who enters in will find
Pasture for his heart and for his mind.
There is no other door indeed than this,
Which opens to eternal, joyful bliss.
      Come, says Jesus, come and enter *me!*

I am the bread of life, so take and eat,
And fill your soul and body with this meat,
Then drink my precious blood which purifies,
And from amongst the dead you will arise.
      Come, says Jesus, come and sup with *me!*

I am the light, now contemplate and see
That love and life do both proceed from me.
Alas! The world prefers the dark of night,
Having eyes, but not possessing sight
      Come, says Jesus, come and see by *me!*

I am the shepherd, sent to save my sheep,
They know my voice and trust in me to keep
Them all in safety, far from angry strife.
It is for them that I laid down my life.
      Come, says Jesus, refuge is in *me!*

I am the vine, of which you are a branch,
May all my grapes be juicy, ripe and stanch
The plant which yields no fruit, I cast away,
And burn it in my fire without delay.
      Come, says Jesus, graft yourself on *me!*

I am the way, the truth, the life for all,
And from my Father's mansion now I call.
As source of life, I hung upon the tree,
Of life and death 'tis I who have the key.
      Come, says Jesus, come and live with *me!*

I am the resurrection, the third day,
For in the tomb, as life, I could not stay.
My death destroyed the chains of death and Hell,
In Heaven's prepared a place for all to dwell.
  Come, says Jesus, come arise with *me!*

Paul of Tracheia

FRIENDS

Friends once so dear and precious have gone and left us all alone.
Thou remains, Your love never falters.
You always care for Your own.
We do not need or want for anything when You are around,
God.
Our rock, refuge and friend, one we can all rely on.
Makes us to be Your faithful servant, Your friend forever.
In our dealings with others Lord make us like unto Thee,
Your true and faithful friend.

Nancy Elliott

VISIONS

I always have visions of grandeur,
I imagine just where I should be,
Surrounded by all things luxurious,
And having my afternoon 'tea'.

Every day could be spent doing nothing,
Or planning my days - who can say?
But for now all I have are my visions,
They just help me to get through the day!

Geraldine McCarthy

I PRAY

My Lord as I pray to You I never make demands,
For as I softly sleep my life is in Your hands.
I know that You will give me guidance in everything I do,
Give me expert tuition to help me follow things through.
There are times when I am weary but I know that You are there,
I can feel Your love beside me and I know You really care.
You give me strength to carry on to find my guiding light,
Be it in the daytime or darkness of the night.
And when my heart is heavy and sometimes feeling sore
I know that You are there to make me smile once more,
So Lord if my life is taken before that I awake,
I pray to You Lord to kiss me and with my soul please take
And walk with me up that heavenly golden stair
To take away any suffering and self despair.
To take me to that special place the one that is above,
Where there is a forever peace and special kind of love.

Stuart Laird

SCOTLAND

This autumn has astounded one and all
Never have the colours been so prominent
In the fall.
I have just come back from Scotland,
Where the countryside is supreme,
Its beauty is a glorious dream,
I loved the rolling hills,
With its picturesque scene,
I know it will soon be a lovely dream.

Mary Tickle

MESSAGES

The plush red rose folded in on itself
says, 'Hide your heart.'
The violet blooming in a wood's shade
says, 'Hide your heart, hide your heart
before it is torn open, before it is trodden.'

But the bird pouring song from the tree above
says, 'Show your heart.'
The knight questing for one golden head
says, show your heart, show your heart:
love alone begets love.

The deer who runs from death's barbed point
says, 'Hide your heart.'
The women who stand on a cold street
say, 'Hide your heart, hide your heart
before it is pierced, before it is sold.'

But the dove crooning on this warm red roof
says, 'Show your heart.'
The man dying at a friend's kiss
says, 'Show your heart, show your heart:
love alone begets love.'

Veronica Zundel

THE GRASS CLIPPING WALTZ

In the garden green
The slashing, mashing machine
Pushed up and down
The garden's velvet gown

Led there in a trance
Spring, summer, autumn dance
To a Briggs and Stratton rhythm
Monotony forgiven

Waltz with a daisy
Over the lions dandy
Four leaves of clover mutter
And sip from cups of butter

Under the trees of apple
The machine I try to grapple
Around the gooseberry, current bushes
Past the plums, their summer blushes

Pour clippings on the compost heap
Gaze over lawn, try not to weep
Many a daisy lost her head
But they'll grow back, while I'm in bed

Ian Tiso

I JUST DID

I woke up this morning and felt joy,
I don't know why I felt joy, *I just did.*
Maybe it's 'cause I thought of yesterday
and all the nice things that we did.

I woke up this morning and felt sad,
I don't know why I felt sad, *I just did.*
Maybe it's 'cause people are starving.
Why are so many lives still wasted?

I woke up this morning and felt laughter,
I don't know why I felt laughter, *I just did.*
Maybe it's because I remember tripping
on that plastic container lid!

I woke up this morning and felt worried,
I don't know why I felt worried, *I just did.*
Maybe it's because I get anxious,
in case there's people I've offended.

I woke up this morning and felt selfish,
I don't know why I felt selfish, *I just did.*
Maybe it's 'cause I didn't share my chocolates,
sometimes I'm such a big kid!

I woke up this morning and felt average,
I don't know why I felt average, *I just did.*
Maybe it's 'cause I'm not top or bottom,
I'm just somewhere in the mid.

I woke up this morning and felt happy
I don't know why I felt happy, *I just did,*
Maybe it's because I'm alive,
As I know I'm definitely not dead!

Jacqueline Tong

NATURE'S MEDICINE

If ever life gets you down,
Walk in a wood and look around,
There's natural medicine to be found,
Follow a river's winding way.
Carpets of bluebell and field of hay,
Turn blackness into a sunny day,
Leaves and flowers of assorted hue.
Walk on earth, damp with dew,
Aromas of bitter-sweet fungi-musk,
Blend with acorn and beechnut husk,
Nature's medicine, all of these,
Squirrels run up into trees,
That sway gently in the breeze.

Hear the trill of a songbird,
The sweetest sound ever heard.
This prescription, a walk in the wood,
Guaranteed to make you feel good.
Not tried it yet? Well you should!
If you try it you will see,
Better medicine could not be,
A prescription that works, natural and free,
It's the one that works for me.

Sheila Walters

THE LOVE OF MY LIFE

What is this wondrous thing called love?
It must be a medicine sent from above
With the power to lift my spirit on high
As unfurling my wings I caress the sky.
My heart is filled with peace and bliss
As I taste the Spirit's sweet heavenly kiss,
For no mortal man makes me feel this way,
It's the love of my life and a brand new day.

A Vellam

RESPECT YOUR ELDERS

That senior citizen
Is surely someone's mother?
Or maybe someone's
Father, sister or brother
And would you like this
Surely done by another
Victimising your own parents
Cruelly by some other
Come on there people -
Let's all get this one right
For it could well be
Your parents tantalised tonight!
It happens all over
And you all know this is true
And it may one day happen
Just to someone like you
So show some respect,
And make sure kids are all told
Respect for senior citizens
They must always uphold
For many of these people
Are defenceless as a child
And it could easily be
Your parents being driven wild.

C R Slater

THE SUN

Burns my lips
Like a lover's kiss
Caresses my shoulders
In a warm embrace

Envelops and relaxes me
In a cloak of warmth
A golden glow enfolds me
When the sun shines

The sun sweetens
The ripening fruit in the garden
Gives life to all things
Turns my white skin pink then brown
And soothes my soul

Diana Price

TIME HEALS

Time is a healer so the saying goes
But whoever really truly knows
You lose that special someone close to your heart.
You never thought a day would come when you had to part.
Kindred Spirits a unique kind of love.
Only sent from the one who is above.
A life snuffed out, too young to die,
How are you supposed to cope and get by?
Your heart has been broken, split in two.
Does anyone really know what you should do?
Grief has no time limit; it's not like a clock,
You cannot turn it on and off like a mental block.
Your heart is such a fragile thing,
Happiness and sadness it can bring
Memories of your loved one crowd your mind day and night.
No one's really noticed your emotional plight,
You dare not cry unless someone hears.
Or sees your crimson face blotched by the tears.
There is no time limit to this pain you feel,
For you, these emotions are very real.
Friends will be there when the time is right,
They will give you hugs and cuddle you tight.
Letting go is sometimes the key.
Let those emotions and tears run free.
Your pain will fade and make it easier to bear.
There are people out there who really do care.

Jo Lodge

REALITY

I cannot see the hand that paints the stamens of a flower,
I cannot hear your laughter or you splashing through a shower.
But I feel in times of trouble, your presence very near,
And when my heart is burdened, you fill me full of cheer.

I cannot see the shadow of your figure on the stair,
I do not know your hand on mine or feel you touch my hair,
But when I am confused and tired, your wisdom comes to me,
And when in pain or sorrow, I feel your sympathy.

I cannot see your hand at work but in every living thing,
The tall trees dark against the sky, the flowers that grow in spring,
I see a glory all divine that comes from your heart of love,
And then I long to be with you in mansions far above.

Margaretta Burt

LEARNING TO PRAY

I come to Jesus with a simple prayer
He shows me, He teaches me, He is there
It is not hard to pray to Him
Just talk to Him and sing a hymn

I call my Lord when I need a chat
And talk to Him of this and that
It's really not hard to pray
Prayer strengthens you through the day

When I started to pray, I struggled to see
And then someone said as clear as could be
You must start with words - a few every day
Before you know it, you're learning to pray

So when you're feeling that nobody cares
Just sit down and talk to the Lord who is there
It's simple to learn how to pray every day
Just open your heart and let love have its way

Catherine Johnston

SECURE IN HIM

Your word encourages us Lord
Not to look back but to look forward;
But on this night we look back
With gratitude for the way You have kept us,
For the joys and sorrows
That have shaped our lives
Which in Your love and wisdom
You ordained.
We look back with regret
For the times when we have disobeyed You,
When we have heard Your voice
And have chosen to ignore it.
We look back with joy
At those times when we have felt
The touch of Your Spirit
On our lives and in our hearts,
And our relationship with You
Has been deepened.
We look back with awe
For we have seen the seasons
Come and go, always in the same order.
For the miracles of new life
We have witnessed,
Natural, physical and spiritual.
Yes Lord, we have so much
For which to give You thanks.
Our hearts are full of gratitude and praise

As we remember,
We're just so glad to be Your children
And know that our times
Are in Your hands,
And that's where You keep us too, Lord
In the hollow of Your hands,
Loved and protected and kept by You.

Mary Davies

Can't Stop Singing

I want to sing about Jesus,
I want to feed on His name.
I want to sing about Jesus the King,
Christ Jesus, God's Son, praise His name.

There are so many songs about Jesus,
It's a wonder they don't sound the same,
If sung from the heart,
He won't mind at all,
He just wants our love, praise His name.

Oh wonderful, wonderful Jesus!
I'm so grateful, so thankful You came,
As God's Son you came without blemish or spot
And died for our sin, praise His name.

You freed me from sin, loving Jesus,
You paid a price I couldn't pay,
You hung on the cross and then conquered death,
To sit at God's side, praise His name.

I could sing all night about Jesus,
I imagine His suffering, His pain,
It's hard to believe you did all that for me,
I'm so thankful, I sing, 'Praise His name'.

Let me give you my life, precious Jesus,
Let me tell everyone that You came,
Let them know they've been saved,
By the price of His blood,
With hands lifted, sing, 'Praise His name'.

Now I have a new life in Jesus,
I feed on the bread of His name,
I give thanks to God for sending His Son,
Christ Jesus, the King, Praise His name.

Mary Ashton

HEARTLAND

There's a place I long to be,
Forever will it call to me.
Peaceful landscape,
Wide, wide sky.
When I'm there, my spirits fly,
Tranquillity of mind and soul.
Graceful willows 'gainst the sky,
Skylarks singing, climbing high,
And the grass beneath my feet
Starred with flowers wild and sweet.
Water standing clear and clean
So must Eden have been . . .

Steeped in legend is this place,
Time and tide cannot erase
Enduring beauty, mystic grace.

Sue Cann

REMEMBER US

Remember us at Christmastide
When you're no longer by our side.
Your friendship was worth more than gold.
Without you, life seems strangely cold.

Remember us when trees are green,
When earth displays her brightest scene
And nests are made in holly trees,
Surrounded by their prickly leaves.

Remember us on a summer's day
When sunshine made you want to stay.
You knew that here, your time had passed
But in your hearts, you made it last.

Remember us in your prayers at night
For we shall pray you're in God's sight.
True friends we've grown to love so strong
But could not keep them here for long.

Rich mem'ries now we have in store;
Without them, life would be so poor.
We're glad that you stopped by, that day;
Our friendship now will always stay.

Hazel Mills

OUR PATRON SAINT

The fields and plains stretched
As far as the eye could see,
With a copse of bushes spreading
In patches over the lea.
Mountains formed the skyline
Of the country all around.
A whine of wings I heard
And looked up to the sky.
A large black shape appeared,
Coming closer as round it flew.
Closer and closer, nearer it came,
Until it's shape was seen,
Dark wings spread out from it,
As it came down to feed.
Sheep, cattle, all the same,
They all make good meals.
People fled to raise some help,
To rid them of this great beast.
In answer to their call appeared,
A knight upon his steed.
Down the lea, along the lanes,
Right to its cave they went,
A challenge roared, the beast came out,
Breathing fire as it emerged,
As our brave knight approached.
Battle raged upon the plain,
As many a blow was laid.
Until at last with mighty stroke,
Into its neck, a thrust was truly made
And down that beast did fall.

Ken Copley

PRAISE GOD

All praise to God who made the sky
The sun and moon and stars on high
The earth and sea and all that lives
For life and love to all He gives.

All praise to Jesus Christ the Son
Who victory o'er death had won
He gave His life on Calvary
That all from sin, shall be set free.

All praise be Thee, O Holy Ghost
For power that came at Pentecost
Praise to the Father, praise the Son
The Holy Godhead. Three in one.

S Cowley

I Believe

I believe one day our Lord shall visit
If not in form, then mind and spirit
I believe that He will set us free
And wash the pain from you and me.

P McIntyre

ALWAYS SEEKING

May I always seek the joys that are waiting there - that in return I may show a smile on my face to the whole world.

Add to the pleasure of life - rather than take away - make friends of everyone - not foes.

Let the words from my own lips be ones that hold a power to heal a broken heart - my hands too - let them reach out - ready to help a troubled living soul restore that one - that they may have a peaceful heart, then in return - share their joy with others on the Earth.
In the haste of a busy life - may we all remember life itself is a free gift that should be valued to Heaven's height and should we have the power to do good. Don't hold back, when we do, we make Heaven's eyes smile with delight and angels sing when they see - the good that is taking place - Amen

R P Scannell

THIS GOD THAT I WORSHIP

This God that I worship from of old
Has turned me from timid to being bold.
He taught me how on His Spirit to lean
Become a Christian, His gentle theme.

This God that I worship, I love so much
He cares for me with a merciful touch.
He carries me over the rocks of life's way
I love Him totally and express it each day.

I find in Him my only hope
This enabling me to cope.
I cannot see Him but He's everywhere
At His creation, I just stop and stare.

Our relationship blossoms as the days go by
He cradles me in His arms if I have the need to cry.
I am so glad I know Him well
He sets me free from my strife-ridden cell.

Denise Shaw

MORNING'S GLORY

The sun that guides the sky at early morning
And wakes each earlybird to sing its song
Awakens my heart at daytime's dawning
To happiness that lasts, the whole day long
It gives me joy in all my being
To hear its glad hooray so full and free
And so I praise, my Lord for all His blessings
And all His bounteous gifts He showers on me
He gives me joy in all my hours of waking
So much love each day He gives to me
And so like every feathered bird at dawning
I sing His praise for all His love
For me.

Joan Winwood

A SONG OF HEAVEN

Patience be like a noble reason,
As God He spots, even our slightest treason.
For such be the very heart of the well-known,
When honour with vicious pride has already grown.
Then it becomes so very easy to transgress,
Thus missing out on real happiness.
For such, know the very heart and soul,
And put us in mind for some control.
Many things are put in our way,
But some day we will have our say
On how many new deeds are to be done.
Hopeful for what tomorrow will bring,
Thus the reason why I happen to sing.

Victor Shaw

GOD

It seems that God goes out of His way
To show us all how much He loves us,
It feels like the sunshine follows the rain,
And it's true that we will never be the same.

The autumn sunset will show you -
All the love in His heart,
As beautiful and pure emotions flow,
Yes! Mankind and the Lord of life -
Will no longer be apart.

God will make a short work of the Earth,
And every soul will see what they're truly worth,
Love will reign in both sky and sea,
As creations glory of glories will be set free.

But forgiveness doesn't come easy for any,
And the cross still is there,
We must deny ourselves - unlike many
And live in this world and take care.

And there is a difference between -
Being forgiven and God forgetting sin,
We can take it all for granted,
But remain Holy within.

Simon P Jones

GROWING OLD

There will come a day when you're feeling old,
When your bones grow weak
And you're feeling cold.
When your eyes grow dim and you start to shake,
You cannot sleep and you lay awake.

This is the time when God is near,
He gives you warmth and allays all fear,
He gives strength to tired limbs,
And clears your mind of all your sins.

Growing old should hold no fears,
When you know that God is near.
God is a friend, a friend indeed
And will be there for your every need.

I E Percival

LIGHT AT THE END OF THE TUNNEL

It's not just another day,
it's the start of a new day.
There is no dark tunnel
because the light at the end is so bright,
it will light anywhere,
even there.
Be thankful for this new day,
each day is a new start.
Make each day your own,
enjoy every living moment,
and be thankful for the light.

Gilly Jones-Croft

NEW BEGINNING

B   eginning of creation new
I   nspire and marvel by one and all
R   adiant, beaming joy of delightful gladness
T   enderly, love forever, fondness
H   armonizing of loving happiness

B   irth to a new production
O   ffspring a giver of life of nature
R   adiant being, of joy, of delight
N   ew beginning, what a wonderful sight

P Brewer

LOVE TO GROW

I can make love to grow.
It grows, wilts, seers and fades away,
Springs up and topples over desiccated on the Earth.
I *will* make love to grow.

One *can* make love to grow.
Plant it, protect it, water and shelter it:
A blade so thin and sharp that it mocks as it appears:
Shrivels in winter asking only to be uprooted.

Protect it, water and shelter it.
Its leaves unsheaved are delicate: handle with care.
Its pale bitter blossom twists to face some other sun.
It sickens.

God can make love to grow.
Protect it, water and shelter it.
Sunlight it needs now and warmth;
A bigger pot, more earth.

It will not die.
It strengthens daily and its perfume grows more sweet.
We must make love to grow.

N Windridge

YOU REMAIN
(Hebrews 1. 10-11)

You remain, what blest assurance,
You who came from Heaven to Earth:
You who are my blest Redeemer,
Died that I might know new birth.

You remain my only Saviour,
Conqueror of sin and death:
Let me ever thank and praise You
Whilst You give me daily breath.

You remain my strength and comfort,
Through the trials that I face:
Things of Earth sometimes disturb me,
But I'm kept by wondrous grace.

You remain my peace in sorrow,
As Your promise I embrace:
To be with me now and always,
Till I see You, face to face.

You remain my rock and refuge,
When my way has lonely been:
You've not left me, nor forsaken,
On Your arms, I often lean.

You remain my hope for Heaven,
Though unworthy I may be:
For You purchased my salvation,
When You died on Calvary.

You remain the one who'll call me,
When my time on Earth is done:
You remain, the world's Redeemer,
Jesus, Saviour, God's own Son.

Thomas T Towler

A NEW HORIZON

It is never too late to start again
For God in his love has given a way,
Despite our fear and doubt and pain
A bright new dawn begins each day.
It is our Christ who received God's dove
Who gives our souls a chance to mend,
To learn afresh the joys of love
And in His presence new days to spend.
The way to move despite our fears
Is inward to our deepest being.
Despite the anguish and the tears
From pains of life He is freeing.
No matter how deep or bad the blemish,
His spirit can reach to heal the past.
He, our souls and bodies will cherish
With gifts of joy and peace that last.
Step out in faith and not in fear
Let go the things that hold us tight,
Reach out and let the Christ come near
And walk afresh in God's true light.

Anton

GOD'S PEACE

If I could reach up towards the zenith
And find the perfect words that heal,
I'd scatter them north, south, east and west
For all the world to feel.

And if these healing words would bring
Your peace to all . . . and not just a few;
Bliss would be mine, for then I'd know . . .
The world at last, loved You.

Blanche Helena Hall

FOR THOSE IN PERIL ON THE SEA

O hear us Lord, when we cry to thee, for those in peril
On the sea. Those mighty waters O God whom thou hast
Commanded not to overstep their mark.

Lord, at times they get restless like a wagging tongue;
Shiftless, like one whose feet is swift to spread slander.

They get angry like a man with no sense, like a man
Who is quickly provoked in His Spirit. They puff up like a
Proud man's heart before His downfall. Like a rich man they
Boast of their power. As like a woman in labour, they writhe
Until they give birth to their fury. They rise ever higher,
Like a man sure of His power, certain of His authority, only
To be toppled and come crashing down, in fountains of
Droplets, like the reckless words from a fool's lips.

They gather together, with a lust for greed, to claim more lives,
Like an unwise dictator who cruelly bears down on his subjects
Without thought or concern for their safety;
Ready to swallow them up like the grave, who is never satisfied,
But hungers for more.

Many are foolish enough to trust in it at all times,
Though the weather forecast may be fair, they may forget that Thy
Mighty waters can be temperamental, like a moody man
Who is given to sudden outbursts of rage! Or that they can
Be enticed by the wind; by a blast from Your nostrils, O God.

The sea is at thy mercy O Lord, for Thou didst make it
And all that dwell therein.

When You command the clouds to weep like one who mourns,
Or send forth Your thunder from Your storehouse, like a bully
Who rumbles out his threats, and summon the lightning to strike
Its mark, like an undeserved curse from a rebel's mouth,
The mighty waters tremble at Your rebuke.

The breakers surge forward like a gang of thugs with evil intent,
Tossing their victims about like tiny fishing vessels to and fro,
Causing them to capsize.

O Lord, my God. Maker of Heaven and Earth. I have read that
Your anger lasts only a moment, but Thy favour lasts a lifetime, and
Thou doest what pleases Thee.

O Lord, may it please Thee to keep those safe who are in peril
Of the sea's wrath, and forgive those who may lack respect towards
God
And to what Thy hands have wrought. We are very ignorant at times
And take things for granted, like the beauty of Thy creation.

Have mercy, O God, and grant the ocean-going vessels safe passage
From port to port, though many may perish. I bring no charge
Against thee O Lord and ask not why? For mankind is puny,
Compared to the awesome power and majesty of God the creator.

Before the mountains were born or You brought forth the Earth
And the world, from everlasting to everlasting, You are God.

I just humbly ask You, O God, to have mercy upon whom you will
Have mercy, of those who are in peril on the Sea.

Thank you Lord
Through Jesus Christ.
Amen

Firecloud

CLOSE COMFORT

There is a place where I can go deep inside of me,
A space reserved for all of time where only I can be,
When I need time to think alone, to put my life in order,
And give my mind the privacy amongst chaos and disorder.

At times I need to contemplate on where I feel I am going,
So when I get angry or feel afraid, no one else is knowing,
Those special times when I can see so many problems clearly,
Where no one else can interfere, I hold those moments dearly.

I feel regret for those I know who cannot find such solace,
Who do not take that inward turn and employ life's hidden bonus,
Each one of us is more understood by ourselves than any other,
It makes more sense for me to hear my own heart and mind uncover.

Pamela Rhodes

THE NIGHT

Do I pierce the night
Of an interior death
When all around appears in bloom

So much a mask
Just for friends
In the silence of my tomb

And Christ can rise
To roll the stone
So heavy in my breast

And not snuff out
This smouldering wick
That needs His promised rest.

Dranóel Yengid

WHY ON EARTH?

Why was I put upon this Earth?
What is the purpose of my birth?
Why me? Why here? Why then? Why now?
These weighty questions, I avow,
Need answers if we're to fulfil
God's function for us, and His will.

God wastes nothing in creation,
So each of us must have vocation.
We're all of one, the human race,
In which each has a part, a place,
Wherein we are all implicated
In the mysterious, complicated
Infrastructure of existence,
In response to nature's insistence.

We all have talents, Scriptures say,
To guide us in which role to play.
To greater or lesser extent
Each follows own peculiar bent.
From genius to the humblest mind,
From kingship to the servant kind,
Leaders, followers, supporters - all
Interdependent, need to call
Upon each other's contributions,
Skills, thoughts, ideas, attributions.

Makers, providers, repairers,
Healers, teachers, clerics, farmers,
Soldiers, artists, scientists, scribes,
Even the most primitive tribes,
Family members, fathers, mothers,
Sons and daughters, sisters, brothers -
Myriads of stitches they add,
Of colour, shape, size, good and bad,

Some short, some long, but every stitch
Counts in the world's vast tapestry, which
Records of peoples past, the histories,
To slowly help reveal the mysteries
Of God's amazing universe.

God gave Man for better or worse,
To try to understand the whole,
Life's gifts of body, mind and soul.

So, what answers to my questions?
I have but offered poor suggestions.

I thank God for the privilege
Of life on Earth, wherein I pledge
To strive to weave a telling thread
In needlework of world's wide spread.

Geoffrey Matthews

THE ANGEL HARP

Let me paint mine scene with these poor words
That mine imagination may sprout
    the finest wings ere soaring to distant lands,
As proud and assur'd as a sovereign eagle
    returning triumphant to its fantastic eyrie;
Let mine within eye gaze without
That all cardinal points shalt stand presently
    reveal'd, known and hail'd familiar;
For within the compass of the breeze
Does pleasant music stir,
Caressing mine ear as a dulcet melody
Trilling softly as a liquid enchantment
    woven, as only larksong may;
So pure a stream of liquid notes
Cascading from on high,
As though an angel's harp were softly strumming
Strumming, to a larksong sigh.

M Dixon

MAKE THE MOST OF IT

The years pass by and we all grow old,
These are the best years or so I am told.
Apart from the loss of memory and the aches and pain,
That are made a lot worse when it does heavily rain.
The eyesight going does not help me to cope,
Apathy in my mind causes me not to vote.
I have lost most of my hair and all of my teeth,
The false ones they have given me will not meet.
And to top it all I do whistle now when I do speak.
I can no longer run in fact I can hardly walk
And the missus says I don't make much sense when I talk.
If these are the best years, I long for the past,
Make the most of your youth and health because they won't last.

Don Goodwin

SOARING

Who says only eagles soar the evening skies?
Witness the lowly pelican in flight.
Never was there a more graceful sight,
Five, then twelve, in line or V form
Cutting the horizon at setting of sun.

Out yonder, midst the incredible
background of glowing gold and red,
flies the solo bird with confident wing,
no need she for following;
flock or alone - the choice lies with you.

Not only do eagles soar to the heights,
Use your wings to alter the course
of your given plight.
When inspiration needs awakening,
look up and see these exceptional birds
gain strength in their sight.
Down goes the sun, sigh,
Tomorrow - fly - run
Dare to be free . . . soar high.

Wilma G Paton

WATCH OVER ME . . .

Her name was Ella
Felt like the morning sun
With her elegant touch
Invisible
But beautiful

For the world was dark
Then painted with hope
I see her smile
In my dreams

Enchanted energy
She watched over me
Completed me
Washed away the burning doubt

I thank my Ella
For protecting me
Her spirit lives on
In someone else I used to be.

Kerry Webber

UNITY

Above the serried ranks
of rejoicing standard-bearers
from all the nations
of the earth,
liveried
with the long, dazzling robes
of the household of God,
floating onwards
together
in triumphant procession,
a closely woven carpet,
emblazoned
as on an undulating palette
of rainbow-colours,
and billowing
in the wind of the Spirit,
banners of love,
truth and justice
proclaim the Messiah's
approaching return
to His people.

Bill Drayton

UNTITLED

Music, music, written in words,
Sounds, sounds, to hear, to hear
God and to God, who is around, around,
To Jesus, to Jesus, he is near, he is near!

Simon Beaumont

DO WE?

Christmas, cool, past snow, that came
Hoary signs, from windows came
Reddened nose with cough it came
In rubbing chest that hot it came
Steaming bowl for nose it came
Trust steam to loose, each ailment that came
Must, hard the time, if no respite came
A loss of joy, meant no happiness came
Suffer great loss, when truth's birthday came

Crackling fire, tree, tinsel, came Christmas
A present feast, for all came Christmas
Morn till night, joy, came Christmas
Explain not truth, why was Christmas?

Geof Farrar

WATER, BLESSED WATER

Dear Lord of all and Prince of Peace
Whose mighty wonders never cease
Let me ask thee, if I can,
'Why do you suffer, poor ignorant man?'

For many years, from the birth of man
There never was a peaceful plan
Just war and fighting from the start
To kill for land, the obvious part.

No one fights for deserts
Or frozen lands of ice
The key to life is water
Which is the source of life.

If every land had water
To make a richer, greener land
Then people would stop fighting
And give Jesus Christ a hand.

With water, food and land for all
To make canals would be the call
Plans by men who put man on the moon
Plans for a new world, hopefully soon.

If only people turned to Him
Jesus' words and all His deeds
A Heaven on Earth would surely come
As water, pure water, fills their many needs.

Albert Brindle

I Pray To God To Bring Peace In The World

Peace is paradise.
If I had my way I would like to bring peace every way.
Peace in England. Peace to all the world. Peace among men
Because peace they do deserve.
Peace in the family, peace should be in every family
Peace with brothers and sisters
Because peace is God's will on this Earth
Peace between parents and children
The young should repent and respect more the parents
After all they generated them
Peace in the streets of England and all the world
Peace and no more war
Jesus said, 'Let there be peace in the Earth.'
But some men forget the words of Jesus and make wars
War brings only death to all of us.
War is evil, there is no justification for wars.
Pray to God for peace, if you all wish for paradise
Prayer does not cost anybody a penny
But you could gain peace on this Earth and paradise on the other side
Peace of the mind will make anybody happy.
'Peace, peace,' said God and Jesus.

Antonio Martorelli

I SAID A PRAYER FOR YOU TODAY

I said a prayer for you today
And know God must have heard -
I felt the answer in my heart
Although He spoke no word.

I didn't ask for wealth or fame,
I knew you wouldn't mind;
I asked Him to send treasures
Of a far more lasting kind.

I asked that He'd be near you,
At the start of each new day,
To grant you health and blessings
And friends to share your way.

I asked for happiness for you
In all things great and small,
But it was His loving care
I prayed the most of all!

Margaret A Greenhalgh

TO LIVE IS CHRIST

Our lives are not our own, we've been bought with a price;
Purchased by the blood of Christ as He lay down His life;
To set us free from bondage and fill us with His power,
so that we might live in victory in this very day and hour.

So help us, Lord, to lay aside each besetting sin,
keeping our eyes on You, our God, and knowing we will win!
As we worship You today from the depths of our hearts,
fill each one with all he needs, as a new week he starts.

Keep us focused on *You*, Lord, never yielding to any fear,
feasting daily on Your Word, as the end of time draws near!
There is nothing sweeter than time spent with You,
Hearing Your voice, and obeying all You call us to.

Your words are very strong, yet also soft and calm,
and after You give discipline, You give a healing balm.
So today we wait earnestly before Your throne,
ready to follow You forever, knowing we're not alone!

M McAlister

EASTERS PAST

Next year I'll be seventy.
In my mind I'm seventeen.
A lot of Easters have gone past,
A lot of life between.

I want to do the things I did
When I was young and able.
But now the only eggs I roll
Are boiled ones, off the table!

One Easter when the kids were small
We found a bunny's home.
I'm glad I didn't step on it
Poor babies all alone.

The children peeped between the grass
To see the little buns.
How gentle were their fingers
That stroked the little ones.

Have children grown more harsh today?
And who must take the blame?
The parents? TV? Computer games?
For nothing is the same.

To stamp upon those little ones
Would be nothing odd today.
'Oh God, please save the children.'
For this is Satan's way,
Of making sure his evil deeds
Continue day to day.

Isobel Laffin

COMING ALIVE

Decay wood,
Cobweb dust.
Cover the bracket fungus.
Woodlouse;
Shy little wood mouse.
Bumblebees nest,
In woodpeckers' drills.
Dead branches,
That have been thrown down;
By winter storms,
Are strewn around.
Trunks of ancient coppice
Awake their winter sleep.
Buds unroll into leaves
Seeks warmer air, what we all seek.

Blackthorn's Good Friday's
Crown of thorns.
With glees, greet each spring,
Day's new dawn.
Forestscape Blackthorn's
Blobs of milk white,
Pussy Willow silver silk.
By the babbling steam
Out of the clay,
Pretty Coltsfoot
Yellow display.
Hornbeam renewal green
Inspire, human's spirits, come alive
Signboards of spring, magnificent scenery.

B Clarke

CONSIDER THE EAGLE

There it is, far above the Earth,
The eagle's nest, fast clinging to that rocky ledge,
Reached by only the true lord of the air.

The fledgling has all he needs to fly away,
Has all the equipment necessary;
Yet the world down below looks unfriendly.
Better, he thinks, stay in his own comfort zone.
The nest is best.

Yet a true eagle, so blessed by the parent,
With all good things laid lovingly at his feet
Must learn the strength and power of his wings;
How can he learn to fly without doing it?

The parent is wise; such security is deceptive.
Time for action, a determined shove,
To plunge the young eagle into the perils below.

Yet he was not abandoned, not left to his fate.
Always the parent was with him, going before
To carry him up again, time after time,
Till at last he could soar, high in the sky,
On the thermals of his salvation.

' . . . like an eagle that stirs up its nest
and hovers over its young,
that spreads its wings to catch them
and carries them on its pinions.'
Deut 32:11.

John Stephens

MOMENTS

Keep the moment when your child is born,
Keep it safe and keep it warm.
Keep the moment, let it be kind,
Each child is a gift for all mankind.

Keep the moment when he opens his eyes,
He sees a world, so big, so bright.
Keep the moment when he sees his mother's face,
First moment of love, first moment of grace.

Keep the moment when he says his first words,
Keep the moment when he says his first prayers.
Let him ride on the wings of freedom's dove
And always fill his life with love.

Keep the moment of his first cry in the night,
Keep the moment when you hold him tight,
Keep the moment when you wipe away his first tears,
Keep the moment when you kiss away his first fears.

Don't let these moments get lost in time,
These moments will sustain you when there are mountains to climb.
So keep these moments, keep them strong,
These moments will last your whole life long.

Malcolm Clark

PRACTICAL FORGIVENESS

Forgiven so now let's forget
thus we table turn
and victims sigh
not so, not fair their cry.

such popular misconception
spreads wide
such thinking is the lie!

business as usual
return to normal
sadly
cannot be

consequences
willed to flow
reaping always
what we sow.

forgiveness fair
provides
restitution, due process
time to heal
reflect, consider, feel.

a reciprocal unfolding
with wise welcome
follow thru
impacting both me and you

forgiveness withheld
sometime delayed
awaits true change of heart
open full, complete
reflective on our part.

Brian Strand

LITTLE BROWN DOG

I wonder if Christ had a little brown dog
All brown and soft like mine
With two long ears, a nose round and wet
And two round eyes so tender that shine.

I'm afraid that He hadn't, because I've been told
How He prayed in the garden alone.
All of His friends and disciples had fled,
Even Peter, the one called 'stone'.

And, oh alas, that little brown dog
With a heart so tender and warm
Would never have left Him to suffer alone
But, creeping right under His arm.

He'd have kissed his dear fingers in agony clasped
In counting all favours, but loss.
He'd never have left Him to suffer alone.
He'd have followed Him right to the Cross.

Marion Storey

When a New Day Dawns

Whisper in the night
Whispers in the night as wind sighs and moans
Drumming out a broken rhythm
Stirring up abandoned litter
Around dilapidated territories
Where few persons roam
A rose bush tossed by the wind
Keeps tapping the windowpane
Rustles of laughter sweeps through the trees
Leaves dancing in the uncontrolled breeze
I, thankful to be indoors for the night
Say a prayer for those in peril
Terrified of moans and whispers
Of the wind in the light
God reigns in Heaven
Land, sea and air
Controlled by God's mighty hand
Be strong in your faith
Whispers in the night will disappear
When a new day dawns.

Frances Gibson

SHOPPING DAY

Gradually we moved out of the gridlock of the supermarket
ahead, a twisted shape
dragged out into the gold morning light
a thick winter coat covered a woman's frail body
as she defiantly went about her business
despite knotted veins that poked like thumbs out of her stockings
seeing this my ice-cold hands seemed a little warmer
and the quiet niggles whispering in my bones disappeared
looking out into the wide open grey areas
of car park glistening in the mid morning light
as the small heap of clothes
proud as an Easter garden
crossed the busy road; leaving an impact
as hard as a fired bullet for me to consider, painfully.

Laurence DE Calvert

YOU GAVE ME LOVE GOD!

You gave me a tongue so I can talk
You gave me legs so I can walk
You gave me *love* God.

You gave me feet so I can stand
You gave me fingers on my hand
You gave me *love* God.

You gave me ears so I can hear
You gave me eyes to cry a tear
You gave me *love* God.

You gave me hands to feel and touch
No more can I ask
You gave me so much
You gave me *love* God.

You gave me a nose to smell all that is nice
You gave me all, you gave me life
You gave me *love* God.

You gave me something deep inside
You gave me *love* that I can't hide
You gave me *love* God.

Linda Roberts

FAITH BRINGS CALM

Everyone has a path to tread
Oft be their hearts bled
But faith has powerful healing
Releasing heart-felt feeling
When life becomes mellow
The heart all aglow

If thee believe
Thou will see
When one feels forlorn
The heart so worn
Faith brings calm
Days filled with charm

When faith dwells within thee
Thy life feels free
Relieving nervous tension
Giving one passion
Faith overcomes sorrow
When one feels low

Faith is accepting
The every day sting
When one is about
And filled with doubt
Faith gives thee merit
Uplifting thy spirit

Keeping faith in thy heart
Ne'er to depart
Keeps one in accord
Ready to go forward
Sharing with others good feeling
That only faith can bring.

Josephine Foreman

THE GARLAND

I will give my God a garland
Of hopes and fears and penitence,
Of things not done and empty hands
And feeble efforts to fulfil
His will.

My garland hangs upon the Cross,
All spiked with thorns to pierce His head.
But yet I beg Him turn His loss
To just a few pale flowers of gain,
To forgive.

Lord, melt away the thorns that cluster there
And change them for a newly budding rose,
That I reflect your sweetness and your care,
Your love for me and all men on the Earth
Eternally.

Daphne Timby

BLESSED QUIETNESS

Quiet as the hush of evening,
Softer than the gentle rain,
Warming as a welcome fire,
Soothing all my fear and pain,
Comes the voice of Christ my Saviour,
Midst the clamour and the din
Of life's ordinary duties
Giving calm and peace within.

Knowing Him can bring true pleasure,
With the joy of sins forgiven,
Blessed with God's eternal treasure,
Moving daily nearer Heaven.
Those who know Him must reveal Him
In their lives from day to day,
Whether by their deeds or manner,
Or the gracious words they say.

Help us Lord to follow closely
In the paths that You have trod,
Using every moment wisely,
Till we reach our blest abode.
Telling all the lost and fearful
Of the wonderful new birth,
Help us by the Holy Spirit
To bring Heaven down to Earth.

Denis G Rathbone

WITH R S THOMAS IN MIND

His words shred faith
To its bare bones.
Bones of pain.
The pain of doubt,
The pain of love,
The pain of looking for certainty.
Reaching out for it;
Then seeing it disappear,
As if like a seed
Blown away by the wind.
But in that seed
Is the source of life,
New life which grows
And flowers in the
Spirit's drenching rain.

Pauline Round

MOTHERING SUNDAY

For the love of a mother, so tender and true,
On this special day, Lord, we give thanks to You.
For her self-sacrifice, guidance and care,
In gratitude now, we bow down in prayer.

On this Mothering Sunday, we thank God above,
For the wonderful gift of a dear mother's love.
For her gentleness, patience and wise counsel too,
Above all, for pointing us upward, to You.

Her gracious example has shown us the way,
To aim for the highest, in living each day.
To overcome sin and strive towards good
And do unto others all that we should.

In joy or in sorrow, her love has been there.
In every experience so willing to share.
For love such as this, with heartfelt emotion,
Humbly, we offer, our grateful devotion.

Eileen Phillis

FAITH - THE PANACEA

Said the jesting doctor to a patient, terminally ill,
'Take this medication and, to repeat, you never will!'
What the doctor gave to humour him was a placebo,
But *faith*, the panacea, did heal the patient in toto!
By *faith* the substance of the thing he hoped for, was achieved;
Faith, tiny as a grain of mustard seed, moveth mountains.
Faith the breastplate, kindles the assurance of God's fountains!
Faith without works, is dead; steadfast *faith* faileth not, but saves,
Faith made him whole with placebo, and to God he gave praise:
Faith shines radiantly brightest in a trusting, childlike heart,
Faith is blurred, if from the God of the Bible, it doth part:
Faith sets the opportunity, fear sees the obstacle,
Faith is the panacea to accomplish the miracle;
Faith overcometh the world - earnestly contend for the *faith*
In the steps of Jesus, the author and finisher of our *faith*.

Welch Jeyaraj Balasingam

HARVEST HOME

Perfectly formed in 1973
you were born: but brain
encephalitis flawed you
forever when barely three
month's old. 'He will die
in childhood,' the doctors said.

In the church
on the hill
they prayed for you today:
Christians remembered Christian.
It is the time of harvest plenty
and you are young and twenty.

By tall, stone columns
in aged wooden pew
I joined in prayers for you:
asked the impossible - a miracle.
It is the time of harvest plenty
and you are young and twenty.

Along the paths
past sacred stones
as trees drop down their leaves
you run - I imagine - a child again.
It is the time of harvest plenty
and you are young and twenty.

Time's sickle raised,
poised its cruel scythe.
Only prayers can stay them
loving mercy your life sustain.
May you see next harvest plenty
a year from now: one and twenty.

Anthony J Brady

THE FIRST BIRTH

In that cold stable behind that crowded inn
A child was born pure and without earthly sin
That holy star shone as it appeared in the dark night sky
That beautiful shaft of light shone there before my eyes

Just like the shepherds I followed that bright lone star
When I reached the stable I could only stand and stare
This amazing scene was there before me, my heart missed a beat
I stood before the holy crib and kissed His mother's holy feet

That star so beautiful covered the stable and the Earth below
The wonder I felt my whole being receive, a strong inner glow
This stable became His palace, the animals bowed to the newborn king
Then I heard this beautiful music when Heaven and Earth began to sing

Thro' the years that passed there are saintly writers who record His
holy birth
How the Prince of Glory came so peaceful to this sinful Earth
The stable and that crowded inn will by grace never fade away
When Heaven and Earth joined in celebration upon that joyful day

I was like the shepherd boy who came to a stable to see a king
Then I met the wise men with their richly present they did bring
The prince of morning glory was called a carpenter's son
The second coming of our beloved King it will be done.

J F Grainger

WHEN JESUS SPEAKS

When Jesus speaks
demons fear the most,
it will clean the dirtiest sesspit
and open the deafest ears,
it will make the blind see.

When Jesus speaks
you can hear angels sing,
it will take away all your sin
and you will feel the forgiveness
upon your heart.

When Jesus speaks
barriers are knocked down,
love is felt
your soul will fly with the eagles,
people will get saved.

When Jesus speaks
his word is done,
fear will be no more
tears stop flowing
and hearts stop aching.

When Jesus speaks
the lightning will strike
and the thunder will roar,
the Earth will stand still
and Hell will be no more.

Chris T Barber

THOUGHT FOR THE DAY

Hatred is blackness
That darkens the mind.
Hatred is a sickness
It leaves you behind.

Calmness is far stronger
Than temper you know,
Calmness keeps you longer
From saying, 'You go.'

Truth is a duty
Which man fails to grasp.
Truth is a duty
But stings like an asp.

Love is that great something
That brings cheer and joy,
Love will ne'er do anything
That God will destroy.

William James Price

GLORIOUS WORLD

I hark for the glad sound,
I hark, watch and pray.
Where is the light my Lord, where is the light?
That peeped through so many times, when I was a child?
Suddenly I realise there are wars and rumours of wars,
The prophesies in Matthew 24 are coming to pass,
I try to find peace, I search and wander around.
The sound of children's laughter that used to be, where is it?
I search but to no avail, to find peace.
I wander to a lonely church, but no, even that is not as they
                                                    were years ago.
When you wandered into a church to pray, the doors
                                                    were open every day.
My heart cries, my soul sighs to my Lord to *save* the world *He* made,
The gospel of the kingdom has been preached all over the world,
But there are so many who do not want to know,
Or to remember that one day, as we all do, we have to face this world.
So we must be saved, receive Jesus Christ into our hearts,
And to try to make the world a happier place.
How can this be? Nothing is happy in this world.
God, so loved the world, that He gave His only begotten Son,
That whosoever believeth in Him shall not perish, but have eternal
                                                    life in Jesus Christ
There are but a few of us who love Him, who gather together each day,
In a little church to pray, to receive His body and blood
And remember that Jesus asked us, to do this in memory of Him,
                                                    who loves us.
At night I see the news and flee to my room with tears in my heart.
My soul grieved knowing that my Lord is crying in His Heaven
I pray for the world, but know that one day,
In the twinkling of an eye, our Lord shall descend from Heaven,
And He will come to gather the elect from the four winds
And I know that happiness will be ours who love Him eternally.

But my heart cries out for those who do not listen,
Oh my Lord, save them all, come soon, *please* come soon,
For this world has now turned from a paradise to an abyss,
Please save our world, send our Saviour promised of old,
Send Him soon to make this world - a glorious world.

Nicky Young

GIFT FROM A CARELESS ANGEL

I dreamed a dream of bygone days,
when fortune smiled and skies were clear.
The clouds rained pearls and rainbows danced
and all the while the world sang joy
in sweetest, purest harmony.

A hand then swept this dream away;
a wingèd figure brushed my ear.
'Upon my box of dreams, it chanced
the clasp fell loose; this pretty toy's
now fallen to eternity.'

The angel spoke in flustered daze
while angel eyes dropped shimmering tears:
'This dream mortals weren't meant to glance;
too weak are mortal hearts to buoy
as yet their souls so dazzlingly.
The timing is not right, you see.

Your mortal eyes and mortal ways
are more inclined to blight with fear
such visions, than with care enhance
each other and your world with joy,
which is your Heavenly decree.'

The angel then, in golden haze
and flutter, vanished, but my ear
by dancing voice was still entranced.
'I cannot let you not enjoy
what you have glimpsed, so take from me
this fragment of infinity.'

Christala Rosina

11TH COMMANDMENT POINT A

See others as you
Wish to be seen yourself, till
You know otherwise OK.

Sid 'de' Knees

NEVER GOODBYE

I heard the call
And then I knew
The time had come
For me and you.

To part!
For just a little while
And please!
Just do it with a smile.

For time is measured only by
The love we've shared!
So there is no need
For us to ever say goodbye.

So let us then remember times
Of sunshine, rivers, trees and flowers
With laughter, dreams
And April showers.

Now you and I
With all our might
Put best foot forward
Into the night.

But darkness it
Will never fall
For love will light
The way for all.

For as we step
Upon that ship
And wave our hands
Remember this!

That friends await us at the harbour
Waving as we come in sight
Sad to leave those behind us
But glad to sail into the light.

Joan May Wills

THE SOLDIER'S VISIT

That dead soldier's soul, where does it fly
Soon after it's laid to heavenly rest?
Does it wonder, feel so lonely, know it's passed the final test.
It doesn't seem to understand, what things it should do next.

Should it ask God, can I quickly go
To see my dearest family and good friends?
And try to make them hear my voice
To try and help, to make good death's amends.

So God said, 'You may visit yes, every now and then
Just try to be a gentle breeze, touching sometimes, when
You know a thought of sadness is passing through my sky
That they will learn and know for sure, you really didn't die.'

That soldiers' soul did travel from Heaven straight to Earth
He knew the ropes, and knew the way, now wings about his girth
He gazed upon his family, so sad and feeling so alone
And wanted to shout out to them, 'I'm here, I've come back home.'

But sadly they wouldn't hear him, their hearts just like a stone
For they are in a different world, not that far eternal home
He cried to see them broken and felt God near to his ground
So breathed a breeze upon them to comfort all around.

They all felt that breeze so warm and gentle
And knew from whom it had been sent
Their hearts there, for a moment, not crucified nor bent
Were happy, joined together with joy not sad lament.

The soldier's soul was happy, returned to its new home
And thanked God for that moment, when hearts were not like stone
His soul did understand now, what it should always do
To breeze upon his family, he loved so well and true.

So if you feel that gentle breeze, drifting around you
Be happy, don't feel sad, let not your soul feel blue
It's your soldier on his new wings of God
Come home - to visit you.

Maureen Westwood O'Hara

LET IT SNOW

We bought a tree to make the house look bright
and fairy lights have filled the room with light.
Some neighbours in our village now have been
to church to sing 'Noel the King of Peace'.

Chorus
Let it snow tonight whilst the moon shines bright,
let it snow for evermore,
there's snowflakes down the country lane
and Jack Frost at the door.
Let it snow tonight whilst the moon shines bright,
let us dream of Christmas Day,
there's Santa down our chimney pot,
as snowflakes dance and play.

The chestnuts pop close by the fireside,
we drink your health this Merry Christmastide.
Some carol singers come to sing a tune,
their silvan voices ring across the room.

Chorus

We sleep in bed and dream of Christmas Day,
as Jesus Christ lay in a crib of hay.
A robin comes to bring some mistletoe,
he sits upon a branch all white with snow.

Chorus

Santa makes his way across the skies,
the snowflakes come to dance before his eyes.
The men have tried to clear the snow away,
but grey clouds show that it is here to stay.

Chorus

Tom Clarke

TOUCHED

Could she
Have known love?
A passive youth she be
Naive in thought
Inexperienced
She dances by the river
Blinded by a shimmering reflection
Lost in her deep brown eyes
She stands firmly by my side
Touches my cold hands
Inspires me so . . .
Perhaps, she knows love
Has felt its touch
As soft as the hands that rock the cradle
Gently a baby sleeps
I dream of love
Lost in deep brown eyes
She stands by my side
Touches me so
I am loved
I am sure she knows love
Though a passive youth she be.

High Priest

JESUS WAS A CARPENTER

Jesus was a carpenter,
Working his way in wood,
Cutting away with knives,
Planing and chiselling,
Till it turned out good,
Here at first do we meet him,
In his father's yard,
For Joseph was a saintly man,
Doing all he could
He furnished pots of wood
Whilst he was working at his lathe,
Jesus cut quite a swathe
With the local neighbourhood
Ever so polite and gentle
Never ever rude
His father would turn something beautiful
Fashioning it out of the crude,
Jesus knew even then
He was to be the saviour of men,
So as he watched his father,
He dared to dream a dream,
Of how he would dine with angels,
And be like the gold of a sunbeam.

Alan Pow

THE PROMISED LAND

But seems for hours in eyes to weep,
And hearts to dry away,
All dreams, where hopes and promises,
In fields they loved to stay.

Where once the years of promises
And fields were passed along,
In dreams, turned hopes and dreams again,
Forever now are gone.

Christopher W Wolfe

INFORMATION

We hope you have enjoyed reading this book - and that you will continue to enjoy it in the coming years.

If you like reading and writing poetry drop us a line, or give us a call, and we'll send you a free information pack.

Write to :-
Triumph House Information
Remus House
Coltsfoot Drive
Peterborough
PE2 9JX
(01733) 898102